THE
TRAINING EVALUATION
POCKETBOOK

By Paul Donovan and John Townsend

Drawings by Phil Hailstone

"This Training Evaluation Pocketbook helps to answer t...
what was the final result of the training? Training shoul...
then the organisation. This book gives practical, step-...
training outcome from direct participant feedback to bo...
Joanne Wiersma, Head Nutrition & Health Academy...

"Insightful, well-researched and most practical... this pocketbook is a treasure for all
training professionals. It contains all the tools you'll... and show how
training contributes to your organisation."
Jérôme Monnier, Country Training Coordinator,

Published by:
Management Pocketbooks Ltd

Laurel House, Station Approach,
Alresford, Hants SO24 9JH, U.K.
Tel: +44 (0)1962 735573
Fax: +44 (0)1962 733637
E-mail: sales@pocketbook.co.uk
Website: www.pocketbook.co.uk

This edition published 2004.
Reprinted 2006, 2008.

© Paul Donovan and John Townsend 2004.

British Library Cataloguing-in-Publication
Data – A catalogue record for this book is
available from the British Library.

ISBN 978 1 903776 23 0

Design, typesetting and
graphics by **efex ltd**.   Printed in U.K.

CONTENTS

CONTENTS

4

1NTRODUCTION

DEFINITION

Training evaluation is the process of finding out whether all the money, time and effort put into designing and delivering training courses or other learning experiences was worth it.

The definition of *worth it* depends on your objectives.

Are you looking for participant satisfaction with the training event or another of the nine outcomes we're going to cover in this pocketbook?

INTRODUCTION

NINE OUTCOMES

In this pocketbook we identify nine outcomes which you can measure to find out whether training has been successful:

 Reaction to training – did they like it?

 Satisfaction with the organisation of a training event (facilities, logistics, meals, etc).

 Knowledge acquisition – did they learn anything?

 Skills improvement – can they do something new or better?

 Attitude shift – have they changed their opinions about something?

 Behaviour change – have they changed their way of doing things following the training?

 Results – how did the training impact on the organisation's key success factors?

 Return on investment – to what extent did the training give back more than it cost?

 Psychological capital – how did the training affect corporate image?

INTRODUCTION

SOURCES

The field of training evaluation has been dominated by a few key contributors. We are unashamedly indebted to Donald Kirkpatrick, whose four levels are the foundation of our nine outcomes.

The following management thinkers and writers have also inspired us in our search to provide training professionals with simple and usable ways to measure the effectiveness of what they do (see also Further Reading on page 94).

- **Jack Phillips** – prolific author on the subject of measuring the return on investment of training programmes
- **Mark Easterby-Smith** – of Lancaster University, top UK writer on the subject, developed a model for looking at the purposes of evaluation
- **Anthony Hamblin** – added a fifth level to Kirkpatrick's four-level model. He included the overall well-being of the firm in terms of profitability and survival
- **N. M. Dixon** – exposed the key problems that emerge from a singular dependence on happy sheets
- **Alliger and Janak** – suggested that research on Kirkpatrick's model did not support causality between levels

INTRODUCTION

KIRKPATRICK'S FOUR LEVELS

In the 1950s, Donald Kirkpatrick first suggested that we should evaluate training by measuring four **levels** of impact:

1. **REACTION** – with end-of-course evaluation forms we can find out how participants reacted to the training.
2. **LEARNING** – we can pre- and post-test participants to measure their learning during the training.
3. **BEHAVIOUR** – three to six months after the training we can follow up with questionnaires to participants and their bosses to find out if they have really changed the way they do things as a result of the training.
4. **RESULTS** – although difficult to prove, we can look for evidence that the training has caused an improvement in the organisation's results.

INTRODUCTION

RIVERS AND TRIBUTARIES

With every day that passes after a training event, it becomes more and more difficult to prove that it was the training that caused people to change.

People are exposed to stimulating learning opportunities all around them. What they see on TV and the internet, or hear from friends and colleagues, may influence their behaviour as much, or more than, what they learn on courses. We've represented all these other influences as tributaries flowing into the 'individual performance river' as it winds its way from the 'training course source' to the 'sea of improved organisational performance'.

Organisations react to a myriad of environmental events – from the actions of their competitors to hurricanes and snowstorms. These are the other rivers you can see on the drawing opposite, flowing into the sea.

We hope this simple analogy will show that 'proving' that better trained employees caused better results is sometimes nearly impossible.

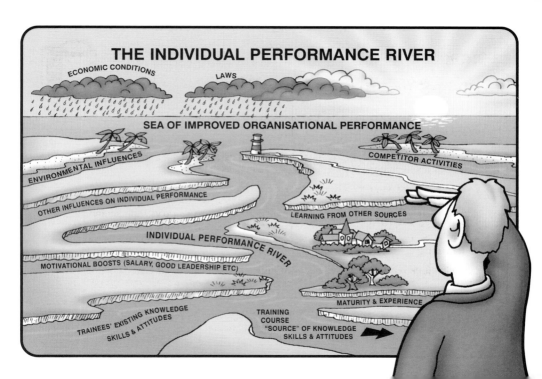

ACCEPTING EVIDENCE

Even though it's difficult to produce scientific **proof** that training causes performance improvement, most managers and other sponsors of training will accept well-presented **evidence**.

As trainers, we should get those sponsors to agree, **before** we deliver training, which of the nine outcomes they will accept as the best evidence that it was successful.

MANAGING TRAINING TRANSFER

Training needs analysis (TNA), training transfer and training evaluation are inextricably bound together. If we trainers want to 'hit the ground running' and make sure we get positive results when we measure any or all of the nine outcomes, then we need to manage (or at least influence) the way in which learning is transferred back to the workplace. In the *Training Needs Analysis Pocketbook*, we have outlined a process to do this called the 8Ps (see over).

INTRODUCTION

MANAGING TRAINING TRANSFER
THE 8Ps

1. **Performance improvement plan** for all employees.

2. **Participation** of line management in design and delivery of training courses.

3. **Pre-course briefings** between participants and their bosses.

4. **Preparation of a learning log** by all course participants to track their progress.

5. **Programme support** from bosses before, during and after the training programme.

6. **Post-course briefings** between participants and their bosses.

7. **Peer and team support** to help implement the learning back on the job.

8. **Prizes and sanctions** for applying the learning to the work.

OUTCOME 1:
REACTION TO TRAINING

OUTCOME 1: REACTION TO TRAINING

INSTRUMENT DESIGN

No surprises here! To measure *Outcome 1: Reaction to Training*, you use a happy sheet, or end-of-course evaluation form.

To keep the information you get from these happy sheets as valid as possible (see also next chapter), we suggest that you keep questions about the training separate from questions about the logistics, facilities, food, etc.

Experience has shown us that, if you don't, then any strong feelings people have about the organisational aspects of the training can spread to their rating of the training itself and pollute the results. That's why we've suggested two end-of-course outcomes to evaluate:

- Reaction to training
- Satisfaction with the organisation of the training

You may even want to go as far as having two happy sheets.

STANDARDS

- It's important not to judge a course too quickly from one set of happy sheets. You need to assess a course over its first few editions and then set an expected standard for the ratings of future offerings. You can then analyse deviations from standard and take corrective action

- You must be aware that different types of courses tend to elicit consistently higher or lower ratings (for example, technical and soft skills courses). Standards should take this into account

DANGER ZONE!

Over 75% of organisations measure participants' reactions to training with happy sheets.

This is far in excess of other measures. Research from the ASTD showed that, in 2002, 44% of US corporations measured how much people learned, only 21% how much people changed their behaviour as a result of training, and a mere 11% measured whether the training affected organisational results.

Herein lies a danger for the quality of training. If participant reaction is the only measure of a trainer's performance, then they will be encouraged to devote too much of their energy to obtaining favourable ratings and not to helping people learn, grow and change.

NO LINK WITH LEARNING

Research studies (including those conducted by Alliger and Janak) have shown that, just because people liked a course, it doesn't necessarily mean that they learned anything.

In fact we even have a suspicion that in some cases the more they liked it, the less they learned!

It's possible that they enjoyed having their mind-set confirmed and not having to move outside their comfort zone.

OUTCOME 1: REACTION TO TRAINING

HAPPY SHEETS

ARGUMENTS FOR

Despite a lot of cynicism about happy sheets there are many reasons to keep using them:

- ✔ Quick
- ✔ Cheap
- ✔ Tell you what's wrong or right about the programme from a participant's viewpoint
- ✔ Usually anonymous
- ✔ Accepted and understood by participants as a tool
- ✔ Indicate to participants a positive and open customer service attitude
- ✔ Help the trainer to determine trends
- ✔ Help the trainer collect a lot of data in a short time
- ✔ Can be used to set standards

OUTCOME 1: REACTION TO TRAINING

HAPPY SHEETS

ARGUMENTS AGAINST

We must not lose sight of some of the downsides of happy sheets:

- ✗ Can be rather superficial
- ✗ Subjective
- ✗ Participants may not always fully understand the purpose of the evaluation
- ✗ Influenced by many variables:
    - personal attractiveness of the trainer
    - amount of enjoyment of exercises and activities
    - timing of sessions/length of breaks, etc
    - soft skills always rate higher than technical courses
    - tendency to allow feelings about one criterion to affect all ratings
    - unwillingness to 'hurt' the trainer with negative ratings/comments
    - end-of-course euphoria

OUTCOME 1: REACTION TO TRAINING

HAPPY SHEETS

DESIGN FEATURES

Experience has shown us that the most effective happy sheet is:

- A form
- Attractive to complete (layout, fonts, colour, etc)
- Easy to understand – unambiguous and clearly laid out
- Short (one page is better than more)
- Computer-friendly (easy to scan/transcribe data)
- Sufficiently spacious to allow for qualitative comments
- Incomplete without a 'Likert' type scale for ratings (ie from 1: very positive to 5: very negative)

HAPPY SHEETS

WHAT TO MEASURE

Overall Evaluation

In order to encourage people to focus on why they came to the training, a good tip is to start the form with a question like:

'Given that these were the course learning objectives....

- *Objective A*
- *Objective B*
- *Objective C*

...what is your overall rating of the learning experience?'

1.	2.	3.	4.	5.

HAPPY SHEETS

FORMULATING THE QUESTIONS

'How did you enjoy this excellent course?'

The person who asked this question possibly had an idea of the kind of answer he/she wanted!

You must be careful to remain neutral in the way you formulate questions and, above all, the rating scales.

A four-rating scale with no 'fence-sitting' middle rating may force people to be more positive or negative than they would have been had they been able to say, '3-medium'. There **is** such a thing as a middle-of-the-road rating and we should give people an opportunity to say so!

HAPPY SHEETS

WHAT TO MEASURE - 1

Here are some of the elements of course performance you might want to evaluate (with neutral, consistently scaled questions):

- Trainer – effectiveness of delivery (voice, eye contact, body language), concern for participants and their learning needs, professionalism in the use of media

- Training methods – a/v equipment, exercise design, 'up-to-dateness', handouts, notes, tangibles (relevance, ease of reference, design, etc)

- Most helpful/least helpful sessions

- Duration

OUTCOME 1: REACTION TO TRAINING

HAPPY SHEETS

WHAT TO MEASURE - 2

- Number of participants (helped or hindered learning?)
- Participant mix (helped or hindered learning?)
- Balance between theory and practice
- Comparison to other courses attended
- Things which caused most/least satisfaction
- Pace of programme
- Perceived level of training
- Suggested improvements
- Recommended for others? (Who?)

Example 1

REACTION LEVEL EVALUATION

For each element of the programme please shade the face which best fits your rating. Brief comments welcome!

Name (Optional) _____

TRANSFORMING THE TRAINER

Theory vs. practice

Least Useful Session? Why?

Usefulness of Documentation

Scope/Length of Programme

Enjoyment & Memorability?

Opportunity to learn from other participants

Extent to which your objectives were met?

OTHER GENERAL COMMENTS (OPTIONAL)

Would you recommend this course to others?

OVERALL EVALUATION OF PROGRAMME

Take-away value to job

Most Useful Session? Why?

Training Equipment (VHF Aids, Talking Walls, TV etc.)

Level/Pace of Programme

Richard as 'Facilitrainer'

Participant Mix (Culture/Level/Age/Background)

Example 2

REACTION LEVEL EVALUATION

Weather report please circle

OBJECTIVES

- To what extent were the objectives of the course clear?
- To what extent were the course objectives met?
- To what extent were YOUR objectives met?

CONTENT

- To what extent was the course relevant to your job?
- Which session was most valuable to you? _____

Why? _____
- Which session was least valuable to you? _____

Why? _____
- To what extent did the exercises support your learning?

28

Example 2

PROCESS

- How do you rate the structure of the course?
- What about the pace?
- To what extent did the course allow you time to practise?

FACILITATOR

- To what extent did the facilitator communicate clearly?
- How knowledgeable did the facilitator seem?
- How well was the facilitator able to demonstrate the skills you needed?
- How well did the facilitator relate the learning to your job satisfaction?

OVERALL

- What's your overall rating of the course?
- How could it be improved? _____

_____

HAPPY SHEETS

HOW TO ADMINISTER

Here are some golden rules about administering the distribution, completion and compilation of reaction evaluation forms:

- Tell the group about the forms at the beginning of the course
- Explain the importance and the pitfalls of this approach
- Consider using 'session-by-session' evaluations if the course is a long one
- Don't ask people to complete the form at the last minute
- Don't encourage participants to confer with each other when completing the forms
- Collect 100% of the responses at the end of the course; don't allow people to send them back later
- Computerise responses, collate data and compare against standards
- Publish results to stakeholders

OUTCOME 2:
SATISFACTION WITH THE
ORGANISATION OF TRAINING

THE SAME AGAIN

Everything we've said about happy sheets applies to satisfaction sheets! As mentioned on page 16 we suggest you separate the evaluation of what people thought of the **training** from what they thought about the way it was **organised**.

WHAT TO MEASURE

PRE-COURSE ELEMENTS

It may be important for you to measure the level of people's satisfaction with:

- Ease of registration
- The training department's response to queries. Information availability (brochures, etc)
- The user-friendliness of joining instructions
- Ease of finding the course location (map provided?)
- The location itself (building, situation, etc)
- Parking (space, accessibility to building, cost, etc)
- Reception (welcome, etc)
- Pre-course refreshments

OUTCOME 2: SATISFACTION WITH THE ORGANISATION

WHAT TO MEASURE

DURING THE COURSE

Because people's rating of 'in-course service' may seriously affect their overall evaluation of the learning experience, you may need to include any or all of the following elements in your satisfaction form:

- Room layout (proportions, height, light, tiered vs flat, quality and modularity of furniture)
- Air-conditioning
- Availability of refreshments
- Proximity of toilets, cloakroom, etc
- Proximity and standard of break-out rooms
- 'Social' space for participants
- Security of personal belongings
- Messaging service and/or availability of email facilities
- Noise levels
- Quality and timing of refreshment breaks
- Quality of food (where applicable)

OUTCOME 3:
KNOWLEDGE ACQUISITION

TESTS

The simplest and most obvious way to evaluate the acquisition of knowledge is with a well-designed test. In fact, some 'compliance' type training courses might be designed solely to allow participants to pass a test and gain certification.

If we want to prove that training caused learning then we need to give a pre-test before the course starts, and the same test at the end – so we can measure the difference in scores.

And if we want to be really scientific about it, we'll even have to consider testing a control group which doesn't get trained! (see page 42).

RECAP QUIZZES

Some trainers prefer quizzes to tests – they're less like school and more fun.
A recap quiz at the beginning or end of each day can quickly test whether the
participants have learned anything. The only limit to designing quizzes for your courses
is your imagination!

Here are some typical recap 'vehicles':

- 'Jeopardy' – here's the answer, what's the question?
- Team A writes questions for team B and vice versa
- Fill in the blanks
- Clustercards (see page 38)
- Recto-verso (see pages 39-40)
- Multiple choice questions
- TV news – teams present a recap of learning in the style of the TV news
- T-shirt recap – teams write learning points on a white T-shirt and present a fashion
  parade to other teams

OUTCOME 3: KNOWLEDGE ACQUISITION

CLUSTERCARDS

Clustercards is a card-based learning evaluation for pairs or trios. It allows them to measure their learning of steps, phases, types or sequences. It's especially effective for technical or procedural courses because it introduces a fun element into what could be a daunting and boring 'test'.

Examples:
- Kirkpatrick's four levels of training evaluation
- The five steps of a sales call
- The features and/or benefits of three to six new products
- The characteristics of four new IT programs or systems
- The four stages of team development
- Phases in the XYZ manufacturing process

HOW? Create a set of four to five cards (including a title card) for each type/phase/step etc. Each card should contain a short description of one of its elements or components (ie four cards each describing a different feature or benefit of three to six new products). Ask pairs or trios of participants to complete the clusters by placing the cards in right order 'clusters' on a table top and award a prize for the first to finish with all cards correctly placed.

RECTO-VERSO: WHAT?

Recto-verso (French for back-to-front printing) is a flashcard-based exercise for pairs or trios to test learning at any time during a course. True/false statements are written on the front and back of a set of 5 to 30 small (A7) cards. It's especially useful on courses with heavy technical content.

Participants are asked to read the cards together and decide which of the two statements (recto or verso) is correct.

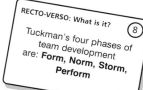

Example:

- FRONT: Tuckman's four phases of team development are: **Form, Norm, Storm, Perform**

- BACK: Tuckman's four phases of team development are: **Form, Storm, Norm, Perform**

NB: Some cards (60%) should be factual (as above) and 40% debatable to provoke a true evaluation of learning.

OUTCOME 3: KNOWLEDGE ACQUISITION

RECTO-VERSO: HOW TO USE IT?

The process for designing and running a recto-verso evaluation is as follows:

- Create between 5 and 30 true/false statements about the subject matter to be tested or reviewed
- Print a **true** statement on one side and the corresponding **false** statement on the other side of a set of small A7 cards. It's useful to have about 40% of them debatable so as to provoke…..debate! *Example: In a role play exercise it's best for the trainer to play the 'challenger' role. In a role play exercise it's best if another participant plays the 'challenger' role*
- Print a hidden code on the cards so you can quickly identify right and wrong answers
- Distribute complete sets of cards to pairs or trios. Ask them to place the correct answer **face up**
- Allow five minutes per 10 cards for team discussion and decision
- Tell them that the **right** answers have the xyz code and ask them to remove all those cards leaving only those with the **wrong** answers on the table
- Ask those teams with **right** answers to try and convince those with **wrong** answers
- If disagreement persists despite your intervention…..tear up the card!

CASE STUDIES

Case studies are descriptions of problems whose solutions require participants to practise and therefore be evaluated on:

- The application of newly acquired knowledge

- Newly learned skills

- The investigation/ demonstration of new attitudes or values

DESIGN

- Decide on knowledge/ skills/attitudes to be developed
- Create or find a 'real' problem
- Write onto a handout, flip or slide; show video; perform sketch
- Identify appropriate solutions
- Prepare questions for the group

DELIVERY

- Explain case to group
- Demonstrate expected results
- Break into groups of 3-7
- Reconvene in plenary
- Encourage different opinions
- Tabulate consensus items
- Add missing items
- **GIVE FEEDBACK**

CONTROL GROUPS

Scientists use control groups if they want to prove that there were no alternative explanations to why something happened. A control group is a group of people who are identical to the group in the experiment but who do **not** participate.

Training purists will tell you that if you want to prove that training causes learning, you have to show that participants could not have got their new knowledge from an alternative source (eg TV, friends, the internet, etc).

To do this you compare the trainees' test results with those of a previously selected (identical) group of people who did **not** follow the training. Then you can declare, they say, that the training (and **only** the training) has made the difference.

One small disadvantage – try explaining that you need a control group to your average general manager!

OUTCOME 4:
SKILLS IMPROVEMENT

OBSERVATION

Skills improvement has to be seen to be believed!

To measure the improvement on a course we need to incorporate exercises which will allow the trainer and/or other participants to observe the new skills being practised. There are several ways to structure this observation process.

The simplest one is for the trainer to ask individuals to perform a task and then observe how s/he does it using a checklist so as to be able to give feedback.

Once feedback has been given, the trainee tries again…..and again…..till s/he gets it right.

Another way is to use a video camera so that the trainee can also observe him/herself. Again, the observer(s) should use a checklist, give feedback, allow a second try, and so on.

ROLE PLAYS
THREE TYPES

Role plays are 'reality practice'. They give participants who have learned a new skill the opportunity to practise using it in a relatively safe environment. With video and/or observer feedback, role play can represent an excellent way of evaluating whether a skill has been acquired or improved. The three types of role play are:

1. UNSTRUCTURED – participants are asked to role play an interactive situation with no behavioural instructions.

2. STRUCTURED – participants are given a rough outline of who should take what position, stand or attitude during the role play.

3. SCRIPTED – participants are given very clear instructions on what to say and do during the role play.

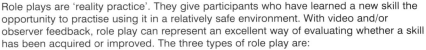

OUTCOME 4: SKILLS IMPROVEMENT

ROLE PLAYS
TEN DESIGN RULES

In order for role play to be accepted as a valid evaluation of skills demonstration, you should follow these few guiding principles:

1. Choose a specific, relevant situation related to the learning objective.
2. Design the level of structure (see previous page) to suit the learning objective.
3. Brief participants early to avoid apprehension. Position the exercise to minimise stress.
4. Allocate roles by encouraging volunteers and ensure they understand what's expected.
5. Occupy the 'audience' productively with observer roles and templates.
6. Set and display ground rules.
7. Maintain 'gravitas' throughout the role play (no interruptions).
8. Rate participants' skills on a prepared checklist of learning objectives.
9. Debrief thoroughly using the learning objectives as an agenda.
10. Encourage supplementary feedback from observers.

OUTCOME 4: SKILLS IMPROVEMENT

ROLE PLAYS

ADVANTAGES AND DISADVANTAGES

FOR ✔

- ✔ Generally exciting
- ✔ Can be 'adrenalin-pumpingly' realistic
- ✔ Learning by doing *par excellence*!
- ✔ Allow participants to experience the effect of an inadequate use of skills in a safe environment (and to observe others experiencing it!)

AGAINST ✘

- ✘ Encourage play-acting
- ✘ Unless the trainer plays the 'challenger' role, learning can be hampered by an unco-operative partner not rewarding good use of skills
- ✘ Not everyone gets to practise every time
- ✘ Participants **can** be terrified by the prospect
- ✘ Debriefing requires sensitivity, skill and experience
- ✘ The audience **can** take a holiday!

ROLE PLAYS

TRIADS

In cases where the number of trainees is too large to permit everyone to participate in plenary role plays, you can split the group into triads with two doers and one observer (rotating?).

Sometimes this can be even more effective than plenary role plays, because the pressure to do well in front of colleagues is less acute.

SIMULATIONS

Simulations are like role play, only more so!

A simulation exercise reproduces, as exactly as possible, the situation and the environment in which a participant will have to demonstrate the skills in question.

Examples:

- In an interactive skills workshop this could mean bringing **real** customers/candidates/suppliers, etc into the training room (John once asked an electrical wholesaler to come for a 'free' lunch during a sales techniques course and be 'visited' not by one, but by ten salesmen one after the other)

- In a presentation skills or train-the-trainer course, participants could be asked to give a **real** presentation or course to the rest of the group

MANAGEMENT AND TEAMBUILDING GAMES

Sometimes a whole range of skills is taught in management and teambuilding workshops, ranging from relatively technical ones like those involved in planning, organising and controlling, to those associated with leadership and interaction with people.

A well-designed and debriefed management or teambuilding game can help people measure their skills – especially if they are video taped. Feedback from the trainer and the other team members can help them gauge their progress and set performance goals.

OUTDOOR TRAINING

More and more organisations are using outdoor training sessions to help trainees practise people and planning skills (bridge building, tree climbing, camping, etc). Detractors say that the only thing these exercises measure is participants' ability to build bridges, climb trees and put up tents.

However, if the experiences are well briefed and debriefed, they can be used to evaluate how well participants can operate in a team under pressure, give feedback to each other and, for those who are put in charge, provide credible, inspirational leadership.

NOTES

OUTCOME 5:
ATTITUDE SHIFT

DEFINITION

We understand an attitude as being the way a person 'leans' towards or against an issue which is of relevance to them, eg company policy, change, management style.

Training sessions are often used by management to attempt to modify employee attitudes. Consequently, evaluation of this type of training will involve trying to measure a shift in attitude.

BEFORE TRAINING

AFTER TRAINING

ATTITUDE SURVEYS: QUESTIONNAIRES

The most common way to measure attitude shift is with a pre- and post-course questionnaire. Here's an example:

What is your attitude towards the new change initiative XYZ?

Strongly against	Against	Neutral	In favour	Strongly in favour

The development of this type of questionnaire requires skill and experience, and might be worth outsourcing since we have to be sure that the questions we ask can and do measure the attitudes we **want** to measure.

ATTITUDE SURVEYS: SPOT CHECKS

A spot check is an easily prepared instrument which can be used at any time before and/or during a training course to measure participants' attitudes for or against any important issue related to the subject of the course.

Participants give their evaluation by sticking a 'spot' (self-adhesive dot), or by making a cross with a marker, on a pre-prepared grid or rating scale. Spot checks can be one or two dimensional.

Examples:

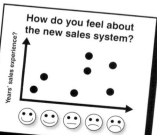

OUTCOME 5: ATTITUDE SHIFT

INTERVIEWS

Some trainers feel that surveys and spot checks don't truly reflect or measure the deeper motivational aspects of individuals' attitudes towards issues and events. They believe that we need to invest time and get as many responses as possible if we want to uncover what's going on under the surface and find out if participants have experienced a shift in their attitude.

For this extra dimension they suggest conducting interviews following a course or other learning experience. Interviews can vary from very structured to very unstructured, but usually the purpose is to let the participant open up and give their true and honest attitude to the issue in question.

It's not usually necessary to conduct a pre- and post-course interview because one well-conducted post-course interview will allow the participant to explain any attitude shift which has taken place since the training.

As the trainer/interviewer, you must take care to position the interview carefully, to relax the interviewee and to offer 'unconditional acceptance' of the opinions expressed.

STRUCTURED INTERVIEW EXAMPLE

'How do you feel about XYZ?'

'Why do you say that?'

'Why is that important to you?'

'How have you changed since...?'

'Why do you think this change has happened?'

OUTCOME 6:
BEHAVIOUR CHANGE

OUTCOME 6: BEHAVIOUR CHANGE

DEFINITION

A behaviour change evaluation is an instrument used to measure whether or not a participant's behaviour has changed as a result of a training experience. The evaluation will usually take place three to twelve months after a training event, depending on how long the trainer and the client/sponsor of the training thinks it will take for new skills to kick in and become anchored in new behaviour.

For example, we may want to evaluate whether sales staff are actually treating customers differently. Are operators using the new quality control procedures? Are managers spending more time with their team members to coach and develop them?

The types of instrument we can use include:

- 90° questionnaires
- 360° surveys
- Observation
- Structured interviews

NO LINK WITH LEARNING!

The bad news for trainers is that, as with reaction and learning, there is no proven link between learning and behaviour change. In other words, just because they learned something doesn't necessarily mean that they will do anything with the learning. We only have to think back to our school days. How much of the stuff we learned in school changed our behaviour?

Just look around at how much training course learning is wasted when people get back to the harsh realities of their jobs. This is why it's worth doing a behaviour change evaluation after many of our courses.....if only because we could save a lot of money if we cancelled some of them!

OUTCOME 6: BEHAVIOUR CHANGE

90° QUESTIONNAIRES

90° questionnaires involve the ex-participant and their boss, as opposed to 360° questionnaires which are sent to people all around (see page 65).

The participant questionnaire is a self-evaluation, where the individual responds to a series of survey questions on the extent to which they have changed their behaviour since the course. The same questionnaire should be completed by the boss. For an example of the wording of these questionnaires see pages 63-64.

NOTE Some trainers tell us that they can't trust people to respond honestly on such a questionnaire. Well, if you can't trust them to reflect honestly on their own or their team member's behaviour, then what can you trust them with?
Besides, if someone says, *'I've changed'*, then the intention is certainly there and has every chance of becoming a self-fulfilling prophecy.

OUTCOME 6: BEHAVIOUR CHANGE

90° QUESTIONNAIRES

> **BEHAVIOUR LEVEL EVALUATION**
> **PARTICIPANT**
>
> *Example*
>
> **COURSE OBJECTIVES:** To analyse, organise and clearly present information in writing.
>
> Use the scale below to answer the following questions.
> Circle only one choice for each question.
>
> | Not at all or Never/Rarely **1** | To a small extent **2** | To a moderate extent **3** | To a great extent **4** | To a very great extent **5** | Not applicable **N/A** |
> |---|---|---|---|---|---|
>
> - To what extent did you use the knowledge and/or skills prior to attending this course?   **1 2 3 4 5 NA**
>
> - To what extent have you had the opportunity to use the knowledge and/or skills presented in this course?   **1 2 3 4 5 NA**
>
> - To what extent have you actually used the knowledge and/or skills presented in this course, after completing the course?   **1 2 3 4 5 NA**
>
> - To what extent has your confidence in using the ...... as a result of this course?   **1 2 3 4 5 NA**

90° QUESTIONNAIRES

BEHAVIOUR LEVEL EVALUATION
SUPERVISOR

Example

COURSE OBJECTIVES: To analyse, organise and clearly present information in writing.

Use the scale below to answer the following questions.
Circle only one choice for each question.

Not at all or Never/Rarely 1	To a small extent 2	To a moderate extent 3	To a great extent 4	To a very great extent 5	Not applicable N/A

- To what extent did s/he use the knowledge and/or skills prior to attending this course?   **1 2 3 4 5 NA**

- To what extent has s/he had the opportunity to use the knowledge and/or skills presented in this course?   **1 2 3 4 5 NA**

- To what extent has s/he actually used the knowledge and/or skills presented in this course, since completing the course?   **1 2 3 4 5 NA**

- To what extent has her/his confidence in using the ... a result of this course?   **1 2 3 4 5 NA**

360° INSTRUMENT

A 360° instrument is a behavioural measure that is completed by people all around an individual (hence 360°) – ie boss, peers, colleagues and subordinates. In completing the instrument these people assess how the participant is performing over a range of behaviours.

When conducted before a training course, and again three to twelve months after, it can provide evidence on how the behaviour has changed as a result of training.

NOTE Although effective, 360° evaluations are time-consuming and relatively expensive.

360° INSTRUMENT

EXAMPLE

How does the person you are scoring rate on the following issue? Please mark an x on the line (1 = Low, 5 = High).

Question 25. **Conducting regular coaching sessions with team members**

1   2   3   4   5

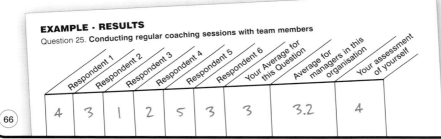

EXAMPLE - RESULTS

Question 25. **Conducting regular coaching sessions with team members**

Respondent 1	Respondent 2	Respondent 3	Respondent 4	Respondent 5	Respondent 6	Your Average for this Question	Average for managers in this organisation	Your assessment of yourself
4	3	1	2	5	3	3	3.2	4

OBSERVATION

Because managers are responsible for the performance (and, usually, payment!) of their team members, they need to be able to monitor that performance – especially when they've invested resources in training them to improve.

Part of this monitoring process involves observation – watching them do their jobs.

However, many people don't like being watched while others like it so much that they start behaving artificially, like in the so-called Hawthorne experiments in Western Electric all those years ago. So it's best to make sure that observation is overt and participatory. The manager should explain how and why the observation is being done, and s/he should always use a template or checklist that gives a clear indication of the required behaviour and the standard that has been set for the job/person.

This template should be developed from the original learning objectives and course content.

OUTCOME 6: BEHAVIOUR CHANGE

INTERVIEW

Just as we saw with attitude shift, we can also evaluate behaviour change following a course, by interviewing participants as soon as enough time has passed to allow new behaviours to kick in.

This kind of interview needs to be structured around the learning objectives of the course, but should also allow latitude for the participants to express their own feelings and beliefs about the skills they covered. It's important that the participants feel relaxed in the company of a non-judgemental interviewer.

The key objective of the interview is to assure the person that it is their evidence that is critical and that you are not looking for any specific responses, nor are you defending the training, nor trying to make them feel guilty if they haven't changed their behaviour.

SAMPLE QUESTIONS
- *'To what degree, if any, has your behaviour changed since the training?'*
- *'If so, why do you think it has changed?'*
- *'How much credit do you give to the training for the change?'*
- *'What relevant behaviours have not changed?'*
- *'Why not?'*

OUTCOME 7:
ORGANISATIONAL RESULTS

WHAT RESULTS?

What we mean by organisational results are those key success factors by which an organisation measures its own progress. Depending on who you work for, these could include:

- Increased productivity
- Fewer industrial disputes
- Better quality of product
- Better public health
- Reduced unemployment
- Cleaner environment
- More sales
- Faster, friendlier service

SCOPE

Only 11% of US corporations tried to measure the impact of training on organisational results in 2002. Why?

- One reason is that the 'individual performance river' – from training course 'source' of knowledge, skills and attitudes to the 'sea of improved organisational performance' – is swollen by many tributaries of other influences (see page 10). It's therefore very difficult to prove that the training caused the results

- Secondly, measuring this outcome is **usually** expensive and time-consuming

But, if you value the benefits of measuring the impact of your training.... read on!

LINKING DESIGN TO RESULTS

INVOLVEMENT OF LINE MANAGEMENT

Measuring the impact of training on results doesn't have to be so difficult or expensive – unless you wait until the training's over. Then it may be too late!

It's a matter of design.

As trainers, we need to create training courses which teach new knowledge, skills and attitudes which, in turn, lead to the achievement of new performance goals. To do this we need to work with senior managers **at the design stage** to quantify what results will be expected from the courses and then, six months later, measure them!

For four specific examples of how to do this see pages 74-75.

SELF-FULFILLING PROPHECIES

Human nature is such that when someone really believes that something is going to happen, they will act in ways that will encourage it to happen, and so it often does.

If trainers and managers really believe that, by training people in XYZ, they will be able to reach new goals, and if they tell these people that they believe it, then everyone involved will probably behave in a way that will facilitate reaching the goals.

In other words they will support the training by making it a priority, follow-up by setting objectives to achieve the new learning and, above all, help trainees eliminate obstacles to reaching these objectives.

LINKING DESIGN TO RESULTS

EXAMPLES

Pharmaceutical Company

PERFORMANCE GOAL	INCREASED PRODUCTIVITY	
TRAINING COURSES	Leadership and Motivation	Business Process Re-engineering
INDICATORS TO BE MEASURED (6-12 months later)	10% less downtime 5% lower absenteeism	€ x000 saving in overtime payments € x000 reduction in overheads

Civil Service (Passport Office)

PERFORMANCE GOAL	FASTER, FRIENDLIER SERVICE	
TRAINING COURSES	Customer Service Skills	ECDL (European Computer Driving Licence)
INDICATORS TO BE MEASURED (6-12 months later)	15% less complaints Waiting time at counter reduced by average of five minutes	Average time from receipt of form reduced by one day Written enquiries answered on average two days faster

LINKING DESIGN TO RESULTS

EXAMPLES

Manufacturing Company

PERFORMANCE GOAL	*BETTER QUALITY PRODUCT*	
TRAINING COURSES	*Quality Improvement Teams Training*	*Statistical Process Control*
INDICATORS TO BE MEASURED (6-12 months later)	*10% more improvement suggestions 5% increase in number of quality improvement projects*	*Quality indicators up by 7% Rejects down by 5%*

Government Department

PERFORMANCE GOAL	*BETTER PUBLIC HEALTH SERVICE*	
TRAINING COURSES	*Performance Management*	*'Promoting health in the community'*
INDICATORS TO BE MEASURED (6-12 months later)	*5% more patients per professional 2% reduction in medical errors*	*2% fewer visits to family doctor for minor ailments 3% reduction in smoking in the area*

CALCULATIONS

On the next page is an example of how one person calculated the specific financial gains from attending a **public** train-the-trainer course at the Master Trainer Institute. Obviously public course outcomes are usually more difficult to measure since the design was not done for a specific organisation.

As you'll see, the calculations are quite spectacular!

RESULTS LEVEL EVALUATION

Example of how one company analysed the savings for ONE YEAR resulting from attending the Master Trainer Programme

Example

	£ Sterling

SAVINGS

Training Needs Analysis
Better analysis of real needs/feasibility of implementing training behaviours resulting in cancellation of ineffective courses.................... £40,000-

Professional Course Design
Better design of courses using accelerated learning techniques resulting in reduction of number of days needed for each course.................... £100,000-

Improved In-house Delivery Competence
Resulting in reduction in number of days outsourced.................... £92,000-

Equipment
More modular training equipment (for example pinboards) resulting in lower hotel and syndicate room costs.................... £18,000-

Employee Motivation
Increased employee motivation following more professional Induction Programmes resulting in 10% less turnover and therefore less days induction training needed.... £30,000-

Sub-total: Savings	£280,000-

GAINS

- Performance Consulting approach results in Management/Trainer synergy so that course content is more driven by topical business concerns. This corporate commitment to training as a way to profit increase creates momentum and 'self-fulfilling prophecy'.
- Pre- and post-course briefs from participants' managers results in 'double' motivation to achieve results.
- Redesign of courses leads to trainees' increased level of skills enabling them to sell HIGHER MARGIN products more easily. Present margin average per salesperson = 2.5%.

If all of the above means ONLY 0.1% increase in average margin to 2.6%.

TOTAL INCREASE	£1,500,000-
	£1,780,000-

COSTS

- 2 New trainers
- New equipment
- Course re-design
- New trainer development....

	£100,000-
TOTAL	£1,680,000-

NOTES

OUTCOME 8:
RETURN ON INVESTMENT

OUTCOME 8: RETURN ON INVESTMENT

DEFINITION

During the 1990s Jack Phillips proposed that trainers go one step further than looking at organisational results as a measure of training impact. He suggested that we have to consider return on investment. In other words, did the training give back more than it cost?

To calculate ROI use the following formula:

$$\frac{\text{Benefits of training programme} - \text{Cost of programme}}{\text{Cost of programme}}$$

To express this as a percentage, multiply by 100!

CALCULATING THE BENEFIT OF TRAINING

When we talk about the benefits of training, we mean the actual money value of the change that training has caused. This implies being able to answer four questions:

1. What is the money value of the performance of trainees **before** the training?

2. What is the money value of the new, changed performance **after** the training?

3. What % of the performance change can honestly be attributed to the training?

4. How much is the % improvement worth?

CALCULATING THE BENEFIT OF 'HARD' SKILLS TRAINING

Whether we work in the private or public sector, it's always possible to put a value on performance improvement.

The market can always tell us how much present performance is worth and, therefore, how much the new, changed performance is worth.

As long as we have identified, at the design stage, the key performance goals expected from the training (see page 72) then we can measure the **before** and **after** performance.

This is relatively easy for courses like sales, safety, welding, maintenance or anything to do with how to make things (extra sales, fewer accidents, less waste, less downtime, fewer rejects, more widgets produced, etc).

CALCULATING THE BENEFIT OF 'SOFT' SKILLS TRAINING

One of the strongest criticisms of ROI outcome measurements is that they don't work for soft skills training.

We suggest that they do, as long as you take the **hypothetical outsourcing** approach to measuring the before and after value of the training. Put very simply, this means:

BEFORE How much would it cost to get this work done at our present level of performance if we were to outsource it to a consultant?

AFTER How much would the desired level of performance cost to outsource?

CALCULATING THE BENEFIT OF 'SOFT' SKILLS TRAINING

Here are some other resources you can use to calculate how much changed performance after soft skills training is worth:

- Senior management/line management/participant estimates

- Industry expert opinion

- Ideas from the organisation's financial controller

- The organisation's past experience with similar training

OUTCOME 8: RETURN ON INVESTMENT

CALCULATING THE BENEFIT OF TRAINING
EXAMPLE

TRAINING COURSE TO BE EVALUATED	*FACILITATING BETTER MEETINGS*	Government Department of Administrative Affairs
VALUE OF 'BEFORE' PERFORMANCE	We can find non-specialized consultants who will facilitate meetings at our present level of competence for €500 per day. Target group = 25 managers. 25 x €500 x number of meetings = €x000	
VALUE OF 'AFTER' PERFORMANCE	25 of our managers can now facilitate meetings at an equivalent specialized consultant's rate of €2000 per day. 25 x €2000 x number of meetings = €x000	
DIFFERENCE	€x000	

ATTRIBUTING PERFORMANCE CHANGE TO TRAINING

With some types of training, most people would not question the fact that the training produced the performance change. For example: accidents decrease after safety training · and rejects decrease after quality training.

With the type of training where it's not so easy, here are six ways to try and estimate the percentage change to attribute to training:

- Post-programme focus groups of specialists and participants

- Interviews with participants and their managers

- Surveys of participants and their managers

- Project assignments following the programme, where participants are required to use their new skills

- Trend-line analyses showing the *direction* of performance over time

- Performance appraisal – people's own assessments on how well they're doing with the new skills and how much of the improvement is due to the training

CALCULATING THE COST OF TRAINING

Here's one way of breaking down the various cost elements involved in the different phases of running a training course:

	Needs Analysis	Design	Development	Delivery	Evaluation
Trainer Costs	X	X	X	X	X
Participant Costs	X			X	
Materials			X	X	
Facilities				X	
Equipment				X	
Other.......					

LIFEBELT

Be careful – some of our more meticulous line manager colleagues may be tempted to scoff at some of our ROI calculations, especially those based on estimates. We can defend ourselves against this criticism by engaging important allies like the organisation's financial controller at the outset.

We should try and get him/her to agree on the basic assumptions underlying the evaluation process.

OUTCOME 9:
PSYCHOLOGICAL CAPITAL

DEFINITION

When we talk about psychological capital we mean:

'The sum of positive opinion about the organisation held by people OUTSIDE the organisation'

OUTCOME 9: PSYCHOLOGICAL CAPITAL

SOCIAL RESPONSIBILITY – A NEW 'CURRENCY'

The world is changing. From Davos and Kyoto, from Seattle, Geneva and Cancun have come protesters challenging the way we run the world today. Every forum, summit and economic conference has to plan for a major protest outside its gates.

A recent article in *The Economist* points out that business is responding to this tidal wave of opinion by asserting that **reputation, integrity and corporate citizenship** matter most.

This may be enlightened self-interest, because the result of emphasizing social responsibility is often an accumulation of psychological capital leading in turn to increased profit.

Whatever the reasons, however, we as trainers cannot ignore this shift. We must ask to what extent our own organisation is taking psychological capital into account when evaluating training. In other words, are we establishing objectives for this outcome at the design stage? (See page 72)

TYPES

Positive opinion about an organisation can be divided into three types, as an answer to the question:

'How is the organisation perceived as ....?'

- **Producer of goods and services** – Brand image? Utility of product? Social acceptability of product?
- **Employer** – Great place to work?
- **Corporate citizen** – Ecological stance and actions? Contributions to charity? Assistance to region/town of implantation? Attitude to corruption?

These are the areas we will want to measure if increased psychological capital is identified as one of the objectives of training.

HOW TO MEASURE CHANGE

What sources of data could we accept as evidence of an increase in our organisation's psychological capital in each of the three areas?

TYPE	EXAMPLES OF SOURCES OF DATA
PRODUCER OF GOODS AND SERVICES	• Baldrige Quality Awards • Egon Ronay/Michelin/Gault et Millaud, etc • ISO 9000 • Brand recognition studies
EMPLOYER	• Fortune 'Best Companies to Work For' Index • European Commission 'Best 100 Employers' • 'Investors in People/Excellence Through People' Awards, etc
CORPORATE CITIZEN	• Dow Jones • FTSE Index of socially responsible companies • Christian Aid report on corporate responsibility

FURTHER READING

New Routes to Evaluation
N.M. Dixon
Training and Development, Vol.50, No.5, Pages 82-86, May 1986

Evaluating Management Development Training and Education
Mark Easterby-Smith, M. Farnborough
Published by Gower Press (2nd Edition)

Evaluation and Control of Training
Anthony Hamblin
Published by McGraw-Hill

Evaluating Training Programs
Donald Kirkpatrick
Published by Berrett-Koehler Inc

Return on Investment in Training and Performance Improvement Programs
Jack Phillips
Published by Butterworth-Heinemann (2nd Edition)